In the Year 1938

by

Kerry Butters

In the Year 1938

Millennium:	**2nd millennium**
Centuries:	19th century – **20th century** – 21st century
Decades:	1900s 1910s 1920s – **1930s** – 1940s 1950s 1960s
Years:	1935 1936 1937 – **1938** – 1939 1940 1941

1938 (MCMXXXVIII) was a common year starting on Saturday (dominical letter B) of the Gregorian calendar, the 1938th year of the Common Era (CE) and *Anno Domini* (AD) designations, the 938th year of the 2nd millennium, the 38th year of the 20th century, and the 9th year of the 1930s decade.

Contents

Events

January

January 20: King Farouk

January 16: Benny Goodman in New York City

- January 1
  - The California Golden Bears defeat the Alabama Crimson Tide in the 1938 Rose Bowl. Final score 13-0.
  - The Company 1938 OEM Industrial Groups was officially registered.
  - The new Constitution of Estonia enters into force, ending the Era of Silence and the authoritarian regime.
  - Sir Alexander Cadogan succeeds Sir Robert Vansittart as permanent under-secretary at the British Foreign Office; Vansittart is "kicked upstairs" by being given the new and

unimportant office of Chief Diplomatic Advisor to the Government.

- o The Merrie Melodies cartoon short *Daffy Duck & Egghead* is released, being the first cartoon to give Daffy Duck his current name, as well as his second appearance.
- January 3 – The March of Dimes is established by Franklin Delano Roosevelt.
- January 12 – The German War Minister Field Marshal Werner von Blomberg marries Eva Gruhn in Berlin; Hermann Göring is best man at the wedding.
- January 16 – Two landmark live recordings are produced this day: the very first of Mahler's Ninth by the Vienna Philharmonic under Bruno Walter in the face of dire circumstance; and Benny Goodman and his orchestra become the first jazz musicians to headline a concert at Carnegie Hall in New York City.
- January 20 – King Farouk of Egypt marries Queen Farida Zulficar in Cairo.
- January 22 – Thornton Wilder's play *Our Town* is performed for the first time anywhere in Princeton, New Jersey. It premieres in New York City on February 4.
- January 25 – A brilliant aurora borealis described variously as "a curtain of fire" and a "huge blood-red beam of light" startles people across Europe and is visible as far south as Gibraltar.
- January 27
  - o The Niagara Bridge at Niagara Falls, New York collapses due to an ice jam.
  - o German War Minister Field Marshal Werner von Blomberg resigns, following the revelation that his new wife had previously posed for pornographic photos.
- January 28 – The first ski tow in America begins operation in Vermont.

January 27: Niagara Bridge collapses in ice.

February

- February 4
  - Adolf Hitler abolishes the War Ministry and creates the Oberkommando der Wehrmacht (High Command of the Armed Forces), giving him direct control of the German military. In addition, Hitler sacks political and military leaders considered unsympathetic to his philosophy or policies. General Werner von Fritsch is forced to resign as Commander of Chief of the German Army following accusations of homosexuality, and replaced by General Walther von Brauchitsch. Foreign Minister Baron Konstantin von Neurath is sacked and replaced by Joachim von Ribbentrop.
  - Walt Disney's *Snow White and the Seven Dwarfs*, the first cel-animated feature in motion picture history, is released in the United States following a premiere the previous year.
- February 6 – Black Sunday at Bondi Beach, Sydney, Australia: 300 swimmers are dragged out to sea in 3 freak waves; 80 lifesavers save all but 5.
- February 10 – Carol II of Romania takes dictatorial powers.
- February 12 – Chancellor Kurt von Schuschnigg of Austria meets Adolf Hitler at Berchtesgaden and, under threat of invasion, is forced to yield to German demands for greater Nazi participation in the Austrian government.
- February 14 – The British naval base at Singapore begins operations.
- February 20 – Sir Anthony Eden resigns as British Foreign Secretary following major disagreements with Prime Minister

Neville Chamberlain over the best policy to follow in regards to Italy, and is succeeded by Lord Halifax.
- February 24 – A nylon bristle toothbrush becomes the first commercial product to be made with nylon yarn.

March

- March 3
    - The Santa Ana River in California spills over its banks during a rainy winter, killing 58 people in Orange County and causing trouble as far inland as Palm Springs.
    - Oil is discovered in Saudi Arabia.
    - Sir Nevile Henderson, British Ambassador to Germany, presents a proposal to Hitler for an international consortium to rule much of Africa (in which Germany would be assigned a leading role) in exchange for a German promise never to resort to war to change her frontiers; Hitler rejects the British offer.
- March 12 – *Anschluss:* German troops occupy Austria; annexation is declared the following day.
- March 14 – French Premier Léon Blum reassures the Czechoslovak government that France will honor its treaty obligations to aid Czechoslovakia in event of German invasion.
- March 15 – Soviet Union announces officially that Nikolai Bukharin has been executed.
- March 17 – Poland presents an ultimatum to Lithuania, to establish normal diplomatic relations that were severed over the Vilnius Region.
- March 18
    - Mexico nationalizes all foreign-owned oil properties within its borders.
    - General Werner von Fritsch is acquitted of charges of homosexuality at his court-martial.
- March 27
    - Italian mathematician Ettore Majorana disappears suddenly under mysterious circumstances while going by ship from Palermo to Naples.

- March 28 – At a meeting with Hitler in Berlin Konrad Henlein is instructed to make increasing demands concerning the status of the Sudetenland but to avoid reaching an agreement with the Czechoslovak authorities.
- March 30 – Italy's *Duce* Benito Mussolini is granted equal power over the Italian military to that of King Victor Emmanuel III as First Marshal of the Empire held exclusively by Victor Emmanuel and Mussolini.

April

- April 10
  - Édouard Daladier becomes prime minister of France. He appoints as Foreign Minister a leading advocate of the policy of appeasement, Georges Bonnet, effectively negating Blum's reassurances of March 14.
  - In a result that astonished even Hitler, the Austrian electorate in a national referendum approved Anschluss by an overwhelming 99.73%.
- April 16 – London and Rome sign an agreement that sees Britain recognise Italian control of Ethiopia in return for an Italian pledge to withdraw all its troops from Spain at the conclusion of the civil war there.
- April 18 – First appearance of Superman (as a backup story), in *Action Comics* #1 (cover date June). The date is established in court documents released during the legal battle over the rights to Superman.
- April 24 – Konstantin Päts becomes the first President of Estonia.
- April 25 – *Erie Railroad Co. v. Tompkins*: The U.S. Supreme Court overturns a century of federal common law.
- April 28 – The towns of Dana, Enfield, Greenwich, and Prescott in Massachusetts are disincorporated to make way for the Quabbin Reservoir.
-

May

- May 5
    - The Vatican recognizes Francisco Franco's government in Spain.
    - General Ludwig Beck, Chief of the German Army's General Staff, submits a memorandum to Hitler opposing *Fall Grün* (Case Green), the plan for a war with Czechoslovakia, under the grounds that Germany is ill-prepared for the world war likely to result from such an attack.
- May 12 – U.S. Secretary of State Cordell Hull rejects Russia's offer of a joint defence pact to counter rise of Nazi Germany.
- May 14 – Chile withdraws from the League of Nations.
- May 17 – *Information Please* debuts on NBC Radio.
- May 19 – May Crisis begins when Czechoslovak intelligence receives reports of menacing German military concentrations. (It later appears the reports were false.)
- May 20 – Czechoslovakia orders a partial mobilization of its armed forces along the German border.
- May 21 – Matsuo Toi kills 30 people in a village in Okayama, Japan, in the Tsuyama massacre, the world's worst spree killing by an individual until 1982.
- May 23 – No evidence of German troop movements against Czechoslovakia is found and May Crisis subsides. Germany is, nevertheless, perceived to have backed down in the face of Czechoslovak mobilization and international diplomatic unity but the issue of the future of the Sudetenland is far from resolved.
- May 25
    - Spanish Civil War: Alicante is bombed by fascist rebels, resulting in 313 deaths.
    - The Soviet ambassador to the United States, A.A. Troyanovsky, declares Moscow ready to defend Czechoslovakia.
- May 28 – In a conference at the Reichs Chancellery, Hitler declares his decision to destroy Czechoslovakia by military force, and orders the immediate mobilization of 96 Wehrmacht divisions.

- May 30 – Hitler issues a revised directive for Case Green - the invasion of Czechoslovakia - to be carried out by 1 October 1938.

June

- June 11 – *Katnip Kollege* is released to theaters.
- June 11 – Fire destroys 214 buildings in Ludza, Latvia.
- June 15 – László Bíró patents the ballpoint pen in Britain.
- June 19 – Italy beats Hungary 4–2 to win the 1938 World Cup.
- June 22 – Heavyweight boxing champion Joe Louis knocks out Max Schmeling in the first round of their rematch at Yankee Stadium in New York City.
- June 23
  - The Civil Aeronautics Act is signed into law, forming the Civil Aeronautics Authority in the United States.
  - Marineland opens near St. Augustine, Florida.
- June 24 – A 450-metric-ton (496-short-ton) meteorite explodes about 12 miles (19 km) above the earth near Chicora, Pennsylvania.
- June 25 – Dr. Douglas Hyde is elected the first President of Ireland.

July

- July – The Mauthausen concentration camp is built in Austria.
- July 3
  - The steam locomotive *Mallard* sets the world speed record for steam by reaching 125.88 mph.
  - The last reunion of the Blue and Gray commemorates the 75th anniversary of the Battle of Gettysburg in Gettysburg, Pennsylvania.
- July 5 – The Non-Intervention Committee reaches an agreement to withdraw all foreign volunteers from the Spanish Civil War. The agreement is respected by most Republican foreign volunteers, notably by those from England and the United States, but is ignored by the governments of Germany and Italy.

- July 6 – The Evian Conference on Refugees is convened in France. No country in Europe is prepared to accept Jews fleeing persecution and the United States will only take 27,370. The prospect for European Jewry looks bleak.
- July 14 – Howard Hughes sets a new record by completing a 91-hour airplane flight around the world.
- July 18 – Wrong Way Corrigan takes off from New York, ostensibly heading for California. He lands in Ireland instead.
- July 22 – Britain rejected a proposal from its ambassador in Berlin, Nevile Henderson, for a four power summit on Czechoslovakia consisting of Britain, France, Germany and the U.S.S.R. London would under no circumstances accept the U.S.S.R. as a diplomatic partner.
- July 24 – First ascent of the Eiger north face.
- July 28
    - A revolt against the Ioannis Metaxas dictatorship is put down in Chania, Greece.
    - *Hawaii Clipper* disappears with six passengers and nine crew en route from Guam to Manila.
- July 30 – The first ever issue of *The Beano* is published.

August

- August – In the face of overwhelming Japanese military pressure, Chiang Kai-shek withdraws his government to Chungking.
- August 3 – Lord Runciman, sent by Neville Chamberlain, arrives in Prague on his Mission of mediation in the Sudetenland dispute.
- August 6 – The Looney Tunes animated short *Porky & Daffy* is released.
- August 10 – At a secret summit with his leading generals, Hitler attacks General Beck's arguments against *Fall Grün*, winning the majority of his senior officers over to his point of view.
- August 18
    - The Thousand Islands Bridge, connecting the United States with Canada, is dedicated by U.S. President Franklin D. Roosevelt.

- Colonel General Ludwig Beck, convinced that Hitler's decision to attack Czechoslovakia will lead to a general European war, resigns his position as Chief of the Army General Staff in protest.
- Ewald von Kleist-Schmenzin arrives in London looking for British support for an anti-Nazi *putsch*, using the looming crisis over the Sudetenland as a pretext. His private mission is dismissed by Neville Chamberlain as unimportant (Chamberlain refers to von Kleist as a "Jacobite"), but he finds a sympathetic if powerless audience in Winston Churchill.
- August 22 – Civil Aeronautics Authority (independent agency).
- August 23 – Hitler, hosting a dinner on board the ocean liner *Patria* in Kiel Bay, tells the Regent of Hungary, Admiral Horthy, that action against Czechoslovakia is imminent and that "he who wants to sit at the table must at least help in the kitchen", a reference to Horthy's designs on Carpathian Ruthenia.
- August 27 – General Beck leaves office as Chief of the General Staff; he is replaced by General Franz Halder.
- August 28 – Lord Runciman's mission to mitigate the Sudetenland crisis begins to break down. British Prime Minister Neville Chamberlain recalls the British Ambassador Nevile Henderson from Berlin, to instruct Henderson to set up a personal meeting between Chamberlain and Hitler.
- August 31 – Winston Churchill, still believing France and Britain mean to honor their promises to defend Czechoslovakia against Nazi aggression, suggests in a personal note to Neville Chamberlain that His Majesty's Government may want to set up a broad international alliance including the United States (specifically mentioning U.S. President Franklin Delano Roosevelt as possibly receptive to the idea) and the Soviet Union.

September

- September – The European crisis over German demands for annexation of the Sudeten borderland of Czechoslovakia heats up.

- September 2 – Soviet Ambassador to Britain Ivan Maisky calls on Winston Churchill, to tell him that Soviet Foreign Commissar Maxim Litvinov has expressed to the French chargé d'affaires in Moscow that the Soviet Union is willing to fight over the territorial integrity of Czechoslovakia.
- September 4 – During the ceremony marking the unveiling of a plaque at Pointe de Grave, France celebrating Franco-American friendship, American Ambassador William Bullitt in a speech states, "France and the United States were united in war and peace", leading to much speculation in the press that if war did break out over Czechoslovakia, then the United States would join the war on the Allied side.
- September 5 – Czechoslovakian President Edvard Beneš invites mid-level representatives of the Sudeten Germans to the Hradčany palace, to tell them he will accept whatever demands they care to make, provided the Sudetenland remains part of the Republic of Czechoslovakia.
- September 6 – What eventually proves to be the last of the "Nuremberg Rallies" begins. It draws worldwide attention because it is widely assumed Hitler, in his closing remarks, will signal whether there will be peace with or war over Czechoslovakia.
- September 7 – *The Times* publishes a lead article which calls on Czechoslovakia to cede the Sudetenland to Germany.
- September 9 – U.S. President Franklin D. Roosevelt disallows the popular interpretation of Bullitt's speech at a press conference at the White House. Roosevelt states it is "100% wrong" the U.S. would join a "stop-Hitler bloc" under any circumstances, and makes it quite clear that in the event of German aggression against Czechoslovakia, the U.S. would remain neutral.
- September 10 – Hermann Göring, in a speech at Nuremberg, calls the Czechs a "miserable pygmy race" who are "harassing the human race." That same evening, Edvard Beneš, President of Czechoslovakia, makes a broadcast in which he appeals for calm.
- September 12 – Hitler makes his much-anticipated closing address at Nuremberg, in which he vehemently attacks the Czech people and President Beneš. American news commentator Hans von

Kaltenborn begins his famous marathon of broadcast bulletins over the CBS Radio Network with a summation of Hitler's address.

- September 13 – The followers of Konrad Henlein begin an armed revolt against the Czechoslovak government in Sudetenland. Martial law is declared and after much bloodshed on both sides order is temporarily restored. Neville Chamberlain personally sends a telegram to Hitler urgently requesting that they both meet.
- September 15 – Neville Chamberlain arrives in Berchtesgaden to begin negotiations with Hitler over the Sudetenland.
- September 16 – Lord Runciman is recalled to London from Prague in order to brief the British government on the situation in the Sudetenland.
- September 17 – Neville Chamberlain returns temporarily to London to confer with his cabinet. The U.S.S.R. Red Army masses along the Ukrainian frontier. Rumania agrees to allow Soviet soldiers free passage across her territory to defend Czechoslovakia.
- September 18
  - During a meeting between Neville Chamberlain and the recently elected Premier of France, Édouard Daladier, and Daladier's Foreign Minister, Georges Bonnet, it becomes apparent neither the British nor the French governments are prepared to go to war over the Sudetenland. The Soviet Union declares it will come to the defence of Czechoslovakia only if France honours her commitment to defend Czechoslovak independence.
  - Mussolini makes a speech in Trieste, Italy where he indicates that Italy is supporting Germany in the Sudeten crisis.
- September 21
  - In the early hours of the day, representatives of the French and British governments call on Czechoslovak President Edvard Beneš to tell him France and Britain will not fight Hitler if he decides to annex the Sudetenland by force. Late in the afternoon the Czechoslovak government capitulates to the French and British demands.
  - Winston Churchill warns of grave consequences to European security if Czechoslovakia is partitioned. The same day,

Soviet Foreign Commissar Maxim Litvinov makes a similar statement in the League of Nations.
- The 1938 New England hurricane strikes Long Island and southern New England, killing over 300 along the Rhode Island shoreline and 600 altogether.
- Following the capitulation of the Czech government to Germany's demands both Poland and Hungary demand slices of Czech territory where their nationals reside.
- September 22
  - Unable to survive the previous day's capitulation to the demands of the English and French governments, Czechoslovak premier Milan Hodža resigns. General Jan Syrový takes his place.
  - Neville Chamberlain arrives in the city of Bad Godesberg for another round of talks with Hitler over the Sudetenland crisis. Hitler raises his demands to include occupation of all German Sudeten territories by October 1. That night after a telephone conference, Chamberlain reverses himself and advises the Czechoslovaks to mobilize.
  - Olsen and Johnson's musical comedy revue *Hellzapoppin* begins its 3-year run on Broadway.
- September 23
  - The Czechoslovak army mobilizes.
  - As the Polish army masses along the Czech border the Soviet Union warns Poland if it crosses the Czech frontier Russia will regard the 1932 non-aggression pact between the two countries void.
- September 24
  - Sir Eric Phipps, British Ambassador to France, reports to London, "all that is best in France is against war, almost at any price", being opposed only by a "small, but noisy and corrupt, war group". Phipps's report creates major doubts about the ability and/or willingness of France to go to war.
  - At 1:30 AM, Adolf Hitler and Neville Chamberlain conclude their talks on the Sudetenland. Chamberlain agrees to take Hitler's demands, codified in the Godesberg Memorandum, personally to the Czech Government. The Czech Government

rejects the demands, as does Chamberlain's own cabinet. The French Government also initially rejects the terms and orders a partial mobilization of the French army.

- September 26 – In a vitriolic speech at Berlin's Sportpalast, Hitler defies the world and implies war with Czechoslovakia will begin at any time.
- September 28 – As his self-imposed October 1 deadline for occupation of the Sudetenland approaches, Adolf Hitler invites Italian Duce Benito Mussolini, French Premier Edourd Deladier, and British Prime Minister Neville Chamberlain to one last conference in Munich. The Czechs themselves are not invited.
- September 29
  - Colonel Graham Christie, former British military attaché in Berlin, is told by Carl Friedrich Goerdeler that the mobilization of the Royal Navy has badly damaged the popularity of the Nazi regime, as the German public realizes that *Fall Grün* is likely to cause a world war.
  - Munich Agreement: German, Italian, British and French leaders agree to German demands regarding annexation of the Sudetenland in Czechoslovakia. The Czechoslovak government is largely excluded from the negotiations and is not a signatory to the agreement.
  - The Republic of Hatay is declared in Syria
- September 30 – Neville Chamberlain returns to Britain from meeting with Adolf Hitler and declares "Peace for our time".

October

- October – The Imperial Japanese Army largely overruns Canton.
- October 1 – German troops march into the Sudetenland. The Polish government gives the Czech government an ultimatum stating that Zaolzie region must be handed over within twenty-four hours. The Czechs have little choice but to comply. Polish forces occupy Zaolzie.
- October 2
  - Tiberias massacre: Arab raiders murder 19 Jewish immigrants.

- Disgusted with Neville Chamberlain's conduct at Munich, Duff Cooper resigns his post as First Lord of the Admiralty. With his resignation, formal debate begins in the Parliament of the United Kingdom on the Munich Agreement, but with Chamberlain at the peak of his popularity, there can be little doubt His Majesty's Government will receive a vote of confidence.
- October 3 – Production of the Jefferson nickel began, replacing the Buffalo nickel (last struck in April 1938). The new nickel was released on November 15, 1938.
- October 4 – The Republican forces in the Spanish Civil War begin withdrawing their foreign volunteers from combat as agreed on July 5.
- October 5
  - Edvard Beneš, president of Czechoslovakia, resigns.
  - In Nazi Germany, Jews' passports were invalidated, and those who needed a passport for emigration purposes were given one marked with the letter J ("Jude" – "Jew").
- October 10 – The Blue Water Bridge opens, connecting Port Huron, Michigan and Sarnia, Ontario.
- October 14 Farah Pahlavi the widow of Mohammad Reza Pahlavi and as such the former Queen of Iran
- October 16 – Winston Churchill, in a broadcast address to the United States, condemns the Munich Agreement as a defeat and calls upon America and western Europe to prepare for armed resistance against Hitler.
- October 18 – The German government expels 12,000 Polish Jews living in Germany; the Polish government accepts 4,000 and refuses admittance to the remaining 8,000, who are forced to live in the no-man's land on the German-Polish frontier.
- October 21 – In direct contravention of the recently signed Munich Agreement, Adolf Hitler circulates among his high command a secret memorandum stating that they should prepare for the "liquidation of the rest of Czechoslovakia" and the occupation of Memel.

- October 24
  - The minimum wage is established by law in the United States.
  - French Foreign Minister Georges Bonnet carries out a major purge of the Qui d'Orsay, sacking or exiling a number of anti-appeasement officials such as Pierre Comert and René Massigli.
  - At a "friendly luncheon" in Berchtesgaden, German foreign minister Joachim von Ribbentrop tells Józef Lipski, the Polish ambassador to Germany, that the Free City of Danzig must return to Germany, that the Germans must be given extraterritorial rights in the Polish Corridor, and that Poland must sign the Anti-Comintern Pact.
- October 27
  - DuPont announces a name for its new synthetic yarn: "nylon".
  - Jews with Polish citizenship are evicted from Nazi Germany.
- October 30 – Orson Welles' radio adaptation of *The War of the Worlds* is broadcast, causing panic in various parts of the United States.
- October 31 – Great Depression: In an effort to try restore investor confidence, the New York Stock Exchange unveils a 15-point program aimed to upgrade protection for the investing public.

November

November 9-10: Night of Broken Glass.

- November 1 – Horse racing: Seabiscuit defeats War Admiral by four lengths in their famous match race at Pimlico Race Course in Baltimore.
- November 2 – Arising from The Munich Agreement Hungary is "awarded" the Felvidek region of South Slovakia and Ruthenia.
- November 4 – At a public meeting in Epping, Winston Churchill narrowly survives an attempt by fellow Conservative and constituent Sir Colin Thornton-Kemsley to remove him from Parliament.
- November 7 – Ernst vom Rath, the Third Secretary at the German Embassy in Paris, is assassinated by Herschel Grynszpan.
- November 9 – Holocaust – Kristallnacht: In Germany, the "night of broken glass" begins as Nazi activists and sympathizers loot and burn Jewish businesses (the all night affair sees 7,500 Jewish businesses destroyed, 267 synagogues burned, 91 Jews killed, and at least 25,000 Jewish men arrested).
- November 10
  - On the eve of Armistice Day, Kate Smith sings Irving Berlin's *God Bless America* for the first time on her weekly radio show.
  - İsmet İnönü becomes the second president of Turkey.
- November 11 – Celâl Bayar forms the new government of Turkey. (10th government; Celal Bayar had served twice as a prime minister)
- November 12 – French Finance Minister Paul Reynaud brings into effect a series of laws aiming at improving French productivity (thus aiming to undo the economic weaknesses which led to Munich), and undoes most of the economic and social laws of the Popular Front.
- November 16
  - The first reported "attack" of the Halifax Slasher mass hysteria incident.
  - Britain formally recognised Italy's control of Ethiopia. In return Mussolini agreed to withdraw 10,000 troops from Spain.
  - LSD is first synthesized by Albert Hofmann from ergotamine at the Sandoz Laboratories in Basel.

- November 18 – Trade union members elect John L. Lewis as the first president of the Congress of Industrial Organizations.
- November 25 – French Foreign Minister Georges Bonnet informs Léon Noël, the French Ambassador to Poland, that France should find an excuse for terminating the 1921 Franco-Polish alliance.
- November 30
    - The Czechoslovak parliament elects Emil Hácha as the new president of Czechoslovakia.
    - Benito Mussolini and his Foreign Minister Count Galeazzo Ciano order "spontaneous" demonstrations in the Italian Chamber of Deputies, demanding that France cede Tunisia, Nice, Corsica and French Somaliland to Italy. This begins an acute crisis in Franco-Italian relations that lasts until March 1939.
    - Corneliu Zelea Codreanu, leader of the Romanian fascist Iron Guard, is murdered on the orders of King Carol II. Officially, Codreanu and the 13 other Iron Guard leaders are "shot while trying to escape".
    - A general strike is called in France by the French Communist Party to protest the laws of November 12.

December

- December – President Roosevelt agrees to loan $25 million to Chiang Kai-shek, cementing the Sino-American relationship and angering the Japanese government.
- December 1 – Slovakia granted the status of an autonomous state under the Catholic priest Fr. Joseph Tiso.
- December 6 – German Foreign Minister Joachim von Ribbentrop visits Paris, where he is allegedly informed by French Foreign Minister Georges Bonnet that France now recognizes all of Eastern Europe as being in Germany's exclusive sphere of influence. Bonnet's alleged statement (Bonnet always denied making the remark) to Ribbentrop is a major factor in German policy in 1939.
- December 11
    - Kingdom of Yugoslavia parliamentary election: The opposition gains votes but not seats.

- o Following elections in the Lithuanian city of Memel the Lithuanian Nazi party wins over 90% of the votes.
- December 13 – The Neuengamme concentration camp opens near Hamburg.
- December 16 – MGM releases its successful film version of Charles Dickens's *A Christmas Carol*. The film is originally intended to star Lionel Barrymore as Ebenezer Scrooge, but Barrymore, ill with arthritis, is replaced by Reginald Owen.
- December 17 – Otto Hahn discovers the nuclear fission of Uranium, the scientific and technological basis of nuclear energy, which marks the beginning of the Atomic Age.
- December 23 – A coelacanth, a fish thought to have been extinct, is caught off the coast of South Africa near Chalumna River.
- December 27 – A massive avalanche of snow hits a construction worker dormitory site in Kurobe, Japan, killing 87.
- December 30 – The ballet *Romeo and Juliet* with music by Prokofiev receives its first full performance at the Mahen Theatre in Brno, Czechoslovakia.

Date unknown

- Establishment of Majlis Khuddam-ul Ahmadiyya by Khalifat-ul Masih II, Mirza Basheer-ud-Din Mahmood Ahmad, the second Caliph of the Ahmadiyya Muslim Community.
- In West Java, Daeng Soetigna tunes the traditional pentatonic angklung to play the diatonic scale.
- Adolf Hitler is *Time* magazine's "Man of the Year", as the most influential person of the year.
- The Walther P38 pistol is introduced in Germany.
- The Schomburgk's deer becomes extinct by this date.
- Herbert E. Ives and G. R. Stilwell execute the Ives–Stilwell experiment, showing that ions radiate at frequencies affected by their motion.
- Family plots produce 22% of all Soviet agricultural produce on only 4% of all cultivated land.
- Women are limited by law to a maximum of 10% of the better-paying jobs in industry and government in Italy.

Births

January

Juan Carlos I of Spain

Teresa del Conde

Beatrix of the Netherlands

- January 1
  - Robert Jankel, British coachbuilder (d. 2005)
  - Frank Langella, American actor
  - Fuad Masum, President of Iraq

- January 2
  - Farouk El-Baz, Egyptian American space scientist
  - Ian Brady, British serial killer
  - Hans Herbjørnsrud, Norwegian author
  - Goh Kun, Mayor of Seoul
  - Dana Ulery, American computer scientist
- January 5 – King Juan Carlos I of Spain
- January 6 – Mario Rodríguez Cobos aka "Silo", Argentine author and spiritualist (d. 2010)
- January 7 – Roland Topor, French illustrator (d. 1997)
- January 8 – Bob Eubanks, American game show host
- January 10
  - Donald Knuth, American mathematician and computer scientist
  - Willie McCovey, American baseball player
- January 11
  - Fischer Black, American economist (d. 1995)
  - Alastair Morton, British railway executive (d. 2004)
- January 12
  - Teresa del Conde, Mexican art critic and historian
  - Lewis Fiander, Australian actor
  - Noel McNamara, Australian justice campaigner and commentator
- January 13
  - Paavo Heininen, Finnish composer
  - Nachi Nozawa, Japanese voice actor (d. 2010)
  - Shivkumar Sharma, Indian musician
  - Daevid Allen, Australian musician (d. 2015)
- January 14
  - Jack Jones, American singer and actor
  - Allen Toussaint, American musician and composer (d. 2015)
  - Morihiro Hosokawa, Prime Minister of Japan
- January 17 – John Bellairs, American writer (d. 1991)
- January 18 – Curt Flood, American baseball player (d. 1997)
- January 20 – Derek Dougan, Northern Irish footballer (d. 2007)
- January 21 – Wolfman Jack, American disc-jockey and actor (d. 1995)

- January 23 – Georg Baselitz, German painter and sculptor
- January 25
  - Etta James, American singer (d. 2012)
  - Shotaro Ishinomori, Japanese author, Father of "Henshin heroes" (d. 1998)
  - Vladimir Vysotsky, Russian singer-songwriter, poet, actor (d. 1980)
- January 28 – Tomas Lindahl, Swedish biochemist, recipient of the Nobel Prize in Chemistry
- January 29 – Shuji Tsurumi, Japanese men's artistic gymnast
- January 30 – Islam Karimov, President of Uzbekistan
- January 31
  - Queen Beatrix of the Netherlands
  - Lynn Carlin, American actress

February

István Szabó

Phil Knight

- February 1 – Sherman Hemsley, American comedian and actor (d. 2012)
- February 2 – Max Alvis, American baseball player
- February 4 – Frank J. Dodd, American businessman and politician, president of the New Jersey Senate (d. 2010)
- February 8 – Prentice Gautt, American football player (d. 2005)
- February 11
    - Bevan Congdon, New Zealand cricketer
    - Simone de Oliveira, Portuguese actress and singer
- February 12 – Judy Blume, American author
- February 13 – Oliver Reed, English actor (d. 1999)
- February 14 – Lee Chamberlin, African-American actress (d. 2014)
- February 16
    - Barry Primus, American actor
    - John Corigliano, American composer
- February 17 – Yvonne Romain, English actress
- February 18 – István Szabó, Hungarian film director
- February 19 – René Muñoz, Cuba-born actor, Mexico-based telenovela/film screenwriter (d. 2000)
- February 24
    - James Farentino, American actor (d. 2012)
    - Phil Knight, American sportswear entrepreneur
- February 25 – Herb Elliott, Australian runner
- February 27 – Jake Thackray, English singer-songwriter (d. 2002)

March

Anthony James Leggett

- March 2 – Ricardo Lagos Escobar, President of Chile
- March 4
    - Angus MacLise, American musician, occultist and calligrapher; drummer for The Velvet Underground (d. 1979)
    - Don Perkins, American football player
    - Paula Prentiss, American actress
- March 7
    - David Baltimore, American biologist, recipient of the Nobel Prize in Physiology or Medicine
    - Janet Guthrie, American race car driver
- March 8 – Bruno Pizzul, Italian sports journalist
- March 9 – Charles Siebert, American actor and director
- March 13 – Erma Franklin, American singer (d. 2002)
- March 14 – Eleanor Bron, English actress
- March 17
    - Rudolf Nureyev, Russian-born dancer and choreographer (d. 1993)
    - Keith Michael Patrick O'Brien, Roman Catholic prelate; Archbishop of Edinburgh
- March 18
    - Shashi Kapoor, Indian actor, director, and producer
    - Charley Pride, American baseball player and country musician
- March 19 – Joe Kapp, American football player and coach
- March 21 – Fritz Pleitgen, German television journalist and author
- March 21 – Luigi Tenco, Italian singer-songwriter (d. 1967)
- March 23 – Maynard Jackson, American mayor of Atlanta, Georgia (d. 2003)
- March 24 – David Irving, English historian and author
- March 25 – Hoyt Axton, American country music singer-songwriter and actor (d. 1999)
- March 26 – Anthony James Leggett, American physicist, Nobel Prize laureate
- March 31 – Joel Godard, American announcer

April

Kofi Annan

Claudia Cardinale

- April 1 – John Quade, American actor (d. 2009)
- April 2 – John Larsson, the 17th General of The Salvation Army
- April 3 – Jeff Barry, American record producer and songwriter
- April 4 – A. Bartlett Giamatti, American president of Yale University and baseball commissioner (d. 1989)
- April 7
    - Jerry Brown, American politician and lawyer, Governor of California
    - Freddie Hubbard, American jazz trumpeter (d. 2008)
    - Jerre Levy, American psychologist
    - Spencer Dryden, American drummer (Jefferson Airplane) (d. 2005)
- April 8 – Kofi Annan, Ghanaian Secretary-General of the United Nations, recipient of the Nobel Peace Prize

- April 10
  - Viktor Chernomyrdin, Russian politician (d. 2010)
  - Don Meredith, American football player and broadcaster (d. 2010)
- April 11
  - Michael Deaver, Reagan Administration Deputy White House Chief of Staff (d. 2007)
  - Kurt Moll, German bass
- April 12 – Roger Caron, Canadian author
- April 13 – Frederic Rzewski, American composer and pianist
- April 15 – Claudia Cardinale, Tunisian-born Italian actress
- April 17 – Kerry Wendell Thornley, American counterculture figure, writer and co-founder of Discordianism (d. 1998)
- April 19 – Stanley Fish, American literary theorist and legal scholar
- April 20 – Tamási Eszter, Hungarian TV announcer and actress (d. 1991)
- April 22
  - Alan Bond, English-born Australian businessman (d. 2015)
  - Issey Miyake, Japanese fashion designer
  - Adam Raphael, English journalist and editor
- April 26
  - Duane Eddy, American musician
  - Maurice Williams, American musician
- April 29
  - Bernard Madoff, American criminal; financial fraudster
  - Larry Niven, American author

May

- May 2 – Paramount Chief Moshoeshoe II of Lesotho (d. 1996)
- May 4 – Tyrone Davis, American singer (d. 2005)
- May 10 – Henry Fambrough, American singer (The Spinners)
- May 11 – Fritz-Albert Popp, German biophysicist
- May 12 – Luana Anders, American actress (d. 1996)
- May 13 – Francine Pascal, American novelist and playwright
- May 17 – Jason Bernard, American actor (d. 1996)

- May 22 – Richard Benjamin, American actor
- May 26
    - William Bolcom, American composer and music arranger
    - Pauline Parker, New Zealand convicted murderer
    - Teresa Stratas, Canadian operatic soprano
- May 28 – Jerry West, American basketball player and executive
- May 30 – Eugene Belliveau, Canadian football defensive lineman
- May 31
    - Johnny Paycheck, American country singer (d. 2003)
    - Peter Yarrow, American singer

June

- June 1 – Khawar Rizvi, Pakistani Poet and Scholar (d. 1981)
- June 5 – Karin Balzer, German athlete
- June 6 – Prince Luiz of Orléans-Braganza, pretender to the Brazilian throne
- June 7 – Goose Gonsoulin, American football player
- June 8 – Mack Vickery, American musician (d. 2004)
- June 12 – Tom Oliver, Australian actor
- June 14 – Shelby Stephenson, American poet
- June 15 – Billy Williams, American baseball player
- June 16 – James Bolam, British actor
- June 19
    - Wahoo McDaniel, American football player and professional wrestler (d. 2002)
    - Ian Smith, Australian actor
- June 21 – Ron Ely, American actor (*Tarzan*)
- June 24 – Abulfaz Elchibey, First democratically elected Azerbaijani president (d.2000)

July

Brian Dennehy

Natalie Wood

Alberto Fujimori

- July 3 – Bolo Yeung, Hong Kong actor
- July 4 – Bill Withers, American singer and songwriter
- July 6
  - Tony Lewis, English cricketer
  - Luana Patten, American actress (d. 1996)

- July 8 – Justin Leiber, American philosopher and science fiction writer.
- July 9 – Brian Dennehy, American actor
- July 10 – Tura Satana, Japanese-born American actress (d. 2011)
- July 12 – Wieger Mensonides, Dutch swimmer
- July 14 – Tommy Vig, Hungarian composer, arranger, vibraphonist
- July 18
  - Ian Stewart, Scottish musician (The Rolling Stones) (d. 1985)
  - Paul Verhoeven, Dutch film director
- July 19 – Jayant Narlikar, Indian astrophysicist
- July 20
  - Roger Hunt, English footballer
  - Dame Diana Rigg, English actress
  - Natalie Wood, American actress (d. 1981)
- July 23
  - Juliet Anderson, American actress (d. 2010)
  - Ronny Cox, American actor
  - Bert Newton, Australian actor and television show host
  - Götz George, German actor
- July 24 – Eugene J. Martin, American painter, artist (d. 2005)
- July 27 – Gary Gygax, American author and game designer (d. 2008)
- July 28
  - Luis Aragonés, Spanish football player and manager (d. 2014)
  - Alberto Fujimori, President of Peru
- July 29
  - Anthony Joseph Burgess, Papua New Guinean Roman Catholic bishop (d. 2013)
  - Peter Jennings, Canadian-born television news reporter (d. 2005)

August

Leonid Kuchma

Kenny Rogers

- August 3 – Sir Terry Wogan, Irish-British radio broadcaster and television presenter/personality (d. 2016)
- August 8
  - Otto Rehhagel, German football player and manager
  - Connie Stevens, American actress, singer and businesswoman
- August 9
  - Leonid Kuchma, President of Ukraine
  - Rod Laver, Australian tennis player
- August 10 – Grit Boettcher, German actress
- August 15 – Janusz A. Zajdel, Polish writer (d. 1985)
- August 16 – Bill Masterton, Canadian hockey player (d. 1968)
- August 19

- o Valentin Mankin, Ukrainian Soviet sailor, Olympic triple champion and silver medalist (d. 2014)
  - o Diana Muldaur, American actress
- August 20 – Alain Vivien, French politician
- August 21 – Kenny Rogers, American country singer
- August 22 – Paul Maguire, American football player
- August 24
  - o Halldór Blöndal, Icelandic politician
  - o David Freiberg, American musician (Quicksilver Messenger Service and Jefferson Starship)
- August 26 – Susan Harrison, American actress
- August 28
  - o Maurizio Costanzo, Italian television news reporter
  - o Paul Martin, 21st Prime Minister of Canada
- August 29 – Robert Rubin, American banker who served as the 70th United States Secretary of the Treasury
- August 31 – Martin Bell, British journalist and politician

September

Romy Schneider

- September 1 – Per Kirkeby, Danish artist
- September 2
  - o Clarence Felder, American actor
  - o Giuliano Gemma, Italian actor (d. 2013)
- September 3 – Ryōji Noyori, Japanese chemist, Nobel Prize laureate
- September 6 – Dennis Oppenheim, American artist (d. 2011)

- September 8 – Kenichi Horie, Japanese adventurer
- September 10 – David Hamilton, British radio and TV personality
- September 13
  - Angus Alan Douglas Douglas-Hamilton, 15th Duke of Hamilton/12th Duke of Brandon (d. 2010)
  - John Smith, Scottish politician (d. 1994)
- September 18 – Poornachandra Tejaswi, Kannada writer (d. 2007)
- September 22 – Gene Mingo, American football player
- September 23
  - Tom Lester, American actor and evangelist
  - Romy Schneider, Austrian actress (d. 1982)
- September 25 – Jonathan Motzfeldt, Prime Minister of Greenland (d. 2010)
- September 28 – Ben E. King, American singer (d. 2015)
- September 29 – Wim Kok, Dutch politician, Prime Minister of the Netherlands from 1994 until 2002

October

Christopher Lloyd

- October 1 – Stella Stevens, American actress and model
- October 3 – Eddie Cochran, American rock 'n' roll singer (d. 1960)
- October 4 – Kurt Wüthrich, Swiss chemist, Nobel Prize laureate
- October 9 – Heinz Fischer, Austrian politician
- October 13 – Christiane Hörbiger, Austrian television and film actress
- October 14
  - Farah Diba, Empress of Iran

- ○ Ron Lancaster, Canadian Football League quarterback and coach (d. 2008)
- October 15 – Fela Kuti, Nigerian musician and activist (d. 1997)
- October 16
  - ○ Carl Gunter, Jr., Louisiana State Representative (d. 1999)
  - ○ Nico, German-American singer (d. 1988)
- October 17 – Evel Knievel, American motorcycle daredevil (d. 2007)
- October 18 – Dawn Wells, American actress
- October 20 – Iain Macmillan, *Abbey Road* photographer (d. 2006)
- October 22 – Christopher Lloyd, American actor
- October 23 – H. John Heinz III, U.S. Senator (d. 1991)
- October 25 – Claude Minière, French essayist and poet
- October 28 – Anne Perry, English-born novelist
- October 29
  - ○ Ralph Bakshi, Israeli cartoonist, film director, and video producer
  - ○ Ellen Johnson Sirleaf, President of Liberia
- October 30 – Ed Lauter, American actor (d. 2013)

November

Queen Sofía of Spain

Ted Turner

- November 2
  - Pat Buchanan, American political operative, journalist, pundit and one-time presidential candidate
  - David Lane, American white nationalist (d. 2007)
  - Queen Sofía of Spain
- November 5
  - Enéas Carneiro, Brazilian politician (d. 2007)
  - Joe Dassin, French singer (d. 1980)
- November 6
  - Mack Jones, American baseball player (d. 2004)
  - Branko Mikasinovich, Serbian-American journalist
- November 10 – Michael Schultz, American film director and producer
- November 11 – Ants Antson, Estonian speed skater (d. 2015)
- November 12 – Benjamin Mkapa, Tanzanian president
- November 13 – Jean Seberg, American actress (d. 1979)
- November 16 – Robert Nozick, American philosopher (d. 2002)
- November 17 – Gordon Lightfoot, Canadian folk singer
- November 19 – Ted Turner, American entrepreneur
- November 24
  - Oscar Robertson, American basketball player
  - Charles Starkweather, American spree killer (d. 1959)
- November 26 – Porter J. Goss, American politician and Central Intelligence Agency director

December

Jon Voight

- December 2 – Luis Artime, Argentine footballer
- December 4
  - Andre V. Marrou, U.S. Presidential candidate
  - Yvonne Minton, Australian soprano
- December 5 – JJ Cale, American singer (d. 2013)
- December 8
  - Ken Delo, American singer
  - John Kofi Agyekum Kufuor, President of Ghana
- December 12 – Connie Francis, American singer and actress
- December 13 – Heino, Ggerman singer
- December 15 – Billy Shaw, American football player
- December 16
  - Frank Deford, American sportswriter
  - Liv Ullmann, Norwegian actress
- December 17
  - Carlo Little, British drummer (d. 2005)
  - Peter Snell, New Zealand athlete
- December 18 – Roger E. Mosley, African-American actor
- December 20 – John Harbison, American composer
- December 22 – Brian Locking, English bassist (The Shadows)
- December 23 – Bob Kahn, American Internet pioneer
- December 24 – Bobby Henrich, American baseball player
- December 25 – Duane Armstrong, American painter

- December 28 – Lagumot Harris, Nauruan politician and President (d. 1999)
- December 29 – Jon Voight, American actor

Date unknown

- Yusuf Lodhi, Pakistani editor and cartoonist (d. 1996)
- Neila Sathyalingam, Singaporean classical Indian dancer, choreographer and instructor

Deaths

January

- January 2 – Henry Victor Deligny, French general (b. 1855)
- January 8
  - Johnny Gruelle, American cartoonist and children's book author (b. 1880)
  - Christian Rohlfs, German painter (b. 1849)
- January 20 – Émile Cohl, French caricaturist and animator (b. 1857)
- January 21 – Georges Méliès, French film director (b. 1861)
- January 28 – Bernd Rosemeyer, German racing driver (b. 1909)
- January 29 – Armando Palacio Valdés, Spanish writer (b. 1853)

February

- February 7 – Harvey Firestone, American tire manufacturer (b. 1868)
- February 10 – Richard A. Whiting, American composer (b. 1890)
- February 11 – Kazimierz Twardowski, Polish philosopher and logician (b. 1866)
- February 18
  - David King Udall, American politician (b. 1851)
  - Leopoldo Lugones, Argentine writer and journalist (b. 1874)
- February 19 – Edmund Landau, German mathematician (b. 1877)

March

- March 1 – Gabriele D'Annunzio, Italian writer, war hero, and politician (b. 1863)
- March 2
  - William Blomfield, New Zealand cartoonist (b. 1866)
  - Ben Harney, American composer and pianist (b. 1871)
- March 12 – Lyda Roberti, Polish actress (b. 1906)
- March 13 – Clarence Darrow, American attorney (b. 1857)
- March 15
  - Alexei Rykov, Premier of Russia and the Soviet Union (b. 1881)
  - Nikolai Bukharin, Soviet politician (b. 1888)
- March 21 – Oscar Apfel, American actor and director (b. 1878)
- March 27 – William Stern, German psychologist and philosopher (b. 1871)

April

- April 1 – Louis-Henri Foreau, French painter (b. 1866)
- April 8 – Joe "King" Oliver, American jazz musician (b. 1885)
- April 12 – Feodor Chaliapin, Russian bass (b. 1873)
- April 14 – Gillis Grafström, Swedish figure skater (b. 1893)
- April 15 – César Vallejo, Peruvian poet (b. 1892)
- April 16 – Steve Bloomer, English footballer (b. 1874)
- April 21 – Allama Iqbal, Indian philosopher and poet (b. 1877)
- April 25 – Aleksander Świętochowski, Polish writer (b. 1849)
- April 26 – Edmund Husserl, Austrian philosopher (b. 1859)

May

Carl von Ossietzky

- May 4 – Carl von Ossietzky, German pacifist, recipient of the Nobel Peace Prize (b. 1889)
- May 9 – Thomas B. Thrige, Danish industrialist (b. 1866)
- May 13 – Charles Édouard Guillaume, French physicist, Nobel Prize laureate (b. 1861)
- May 16 – Lewis Bayly, British admiral (b. 1857)
- May 23 – Frederick Ruple, American painter (b. 1871)
- May 22 – William Glackens, American painter (b. 1870)
- May 26 – John Jacob Abel, American pharmacologist (b. 1857)

June

Ernst Ludwig Kirchner

- June 15 – Ernst Ludwig Kirchner, German painter (b. 1880)
- June 26 – James Weldon Johnson, American author, politician, and diplomat (b. 1871)
- June 29 – Frederick William Vanderbilt, American railway magnate (b. 1856)

July

- July 4
  - Otto Bauer, Austrian Social Democratic politician (b. 1881)
  - Suzanne Lenglen, French tennis champion (b. 1899)
  - Archibald Berkeley Milne, British admiral (b. 1855)
- July 9 – Benjamin N. Cardozo, United States Supreme Court Justice (b. 1870)
- July 17 – Robert Wiene, German director (b. 1873)
- July 28 – Yakov Alksnis, Soviet aviator and commander of Red Army Air Forces (executed) (b. 1897)

August

- August 1 – Edmund Charles Tarbell, American artist (b. 1862)
- August 4 – Pearl White, American actress (b. 1889)
- August 6 – Warner Oland, Swedish actor (b. 1879)
- August 7 – Konstantin Stanislavsky, Russian theatre practitioner (b. 1863)
- August 14 – Hugh Trumble, Australian test cricketer (b. 1876)
- August 16 – Robert Johnson, American blues singer (b. 1911)
- August 29 – Béla Kun, Hungarian Communist leader (b. 1886)

September

- September 1 – Nikolai Bryukhanov, Soviet statesman and political figure who served as People's Commissar of Finances (b. 1878)
- September 15 – Thomas Wolfe, American author (b. 1900)
- September 17 – Bruno Jasieński, Polish poet (b. 1901)
- September 19 – Pauline Frederick, American stage & screen actress, (b. 1883)
- September 25 – Paul Olaf Bodding, Norwegian missionary to India and creator of the Santali Latin alphabet (b. 1865)
- September 28 – Con Conrad, American composer (b. 1891)

October

Ernst Barlach

- October 2 – Alexandru Averescu, Romanian soldier and politician, former Prime Minister (b. 1859)
- October 4 – José Luis Tejada Sorzano, 40th President of Bolivia (b. 1882)

- October 5
  - Faustina Kowalska, Polish saint, the *Secretary of Divine Mercy* (b. 1905)
  - Albert Ranft, Swedish theatre director and actor (b 1858)
- October 13 – E. C. Segar, American comics artist and creator of Popeye (b. 1894)
- October 17 – Karl Kautsky, Austrian Marxist theoretician (b. 1854)
- October 22 – May Irwin, Canadian actress and singer (b. 1862)
- October 24 – Ernst Barlach, German sculptor and poet (b. 1870)
- October 25 – Alfonsina Storni, Argentine poet (b. 1892)
- October 27
  - Lascelles Abercrombie, English poet and critic (b. 1881)
  - Alma Gluck, American soprano (b. 1884)
- October 28 – Fred Kohler, American actor (b. 1888)
- October 30 – Robert Woolsey, American film comedian (b. 1888)

November

- November 1 – Charles Weeghman, American restaurateur and owner of Chicago Cubs (b. 1874)
- November 4 – Samuel W. Bryant, American admiral (b. 1877)
- November 9
  - Vasily Blyukher, Soviet military commander (b. 1889)
  - Ernst vom Rath, German diplomat (b. 1909)
- November 10 – Mustafa Kemal Atatürk, founder of Turkey (b. 1881)
- November 20 – Maud of Wales, queen of Haakon VII of Norway (b. 1869)
- November 22 – Sahachiro Hata, Japanese bacteriologist (b. 1873)
- November 25 – Otto von Lossow, Bavarian and German general (b. 1868)
- November 30 – Corneliu Zelea Codreanu, Romanian fascist, leader of the Iron Guard (executed along other Guard activists) (b. 1899)

December

- December 11 – Christian Lous Lange, Norwegian pacifist, recipient of the Nobel Peace Prize (b. 1869)
- December 20 – Annie Armstrong, American missionary leader (b. 1850)
- December 25 – Karel Čapek, Czech author (b. 1890)
- December 27 – Osip Mandelstam, Russian poet (b. 1891)
- December 28 – Florence Lawrence, Canadian actress (b. 1886)

Date unknown

- Harry Grant Dart, American cartoonist (b. 1869)

Nobel Prizes

- Physics – Enrico Fermi
- Chemistry – Richard Kuhn
- Physiology or Medicine – Corneille Jean François Heymans
- Literature – Pearl S. Buck
- Peace – Nansen International Office for Refugees, Geneva

In the News

Seabiscuit and War Admiral have their long awaited race to decide the best horse in which Seabiscuit beats War Admiral in the race of the Century.

Orson Welles's radio adaptation of The War of the Worlds is broadcast, causing mass panic in the eastern United States.

Germany begins its persecution of Jews.

Freak Waves at Bondi Beach, Sydney, Australia cause 300 swimmers to be dragged out to sea.

Honeymoon Bridge across Niagara Falls, collapses.

German troops enter Austria.

Howard Hughes sets a new Round The World Record of 3 days, 19 hours.

A 450 metric ton meteorite struck the earth in an empty field near Chicora, Pennsylvania.

Oil is discovered in Saudi Arabia.

Inventions Ballpoint Pen, Photocopier, Freeze Dried Coffee.